COLD BLUE STEEL

SARAH CORTEZ

Texas Review Press
Huntsville, Texas

FIRST EDITION, 2013
Requests for permission to reproduce material from this work should be
sent to:

Permissions
Texas Review Press
English Department
Sam Houston State University
Huntsville, TX 77341-2146

Acknowledgements:

Di-verse-ci-ty: 2006 Anthology of the Austin Internation Poetry Festival
J Journal
San Pedro River Review
Lineup: Poems on Crime
Louisiana Literature: A Review of Literature and the Humanities
New Texas
Off the Cuffs: Poetry by and about the Police (Soft Skull Press)
Rattle: Poetry for the 21st Century
Taking Action (Great Books Foundation)
The Weight of Addition: an Anthology of Texas Poetry (Mutabilis Press)

Cover design by Nancy Parsons, Graphic Design Group

Library of Congress Cataloging-in-Publication Data

Cortez, Sarah.
  [Poems. Selections]
  Cold blue steel / Sarah Cortez. -- First edition.
     pages cm
  Summary: Fify lyric poems set in the world of the urban street cop in
Houston, Texas, the nation's fourth largest metropolis -- Provided by
publisher.
  ISBN 978-1-937875-02-2 (pbk. : alk. paper)
  1. Police--Texas--Houston--Poetry. I. Title.
  PS3553.O7227C65 2013
  811'.54--dc23
                              2013001342

811
C

For Larry D. Thomas,
who re-lit the flame

Table of Contents

Section One: Showing Rookies How It Happens Quickly

Section Two: The Inches That Matter to Me

Section Three: Feeling Too Much, At Times

Showing Rookies How It Happens Quickly

AFTER THE SWEARING-IN

Girls,
the badge
is the prettiest piece
of metal you'll ever wear.
Now, you're wedded
to a job
requiring every ounce
of grit you have and then
some. And the odds
are all against you.
Still.

Men,
the badge
gives you the right
to do a job. That's
it. No horse-playing,
sleeping on duty, or
blow jobs in the back seat
of your patrol car. Not
the front seat either.
Dammit.

Officers,
you are now part
of the long and honorable
tradition of Texas
law enforcement. Our
great state is entrusting you
to do what it takes—
legally—to stop the turds.
If you get killed, we'll
bury you with honors. If

you screw up, we'll fire you. If
you keep your nose clean and do
a decent job, you'll probably get
passed over for promotion 'cause the lazy
suck-ups back at the station
will get promoted first. So, do the job
only because you love the job, and
you love justice, and you don't
mind working weekends and holidays
when everyone else in America
is having a good time with friends,
chowing down hot grub. But remember,
boys and girls, Lady Justice is blind,
and she don't see you either.

Good luck to you all.

YOU'LL LEARN

I. Every
one
lies
to
the
cops.

II. Disappointment
prefigures
death.

III. Maggots
bite
hard.

IV. No
one
merits
trust.

V. Ass-hole
is
hyphenated;
cocksucker
is
one
word.

VI. Desire
is
a
bauble.

VII. One
oasis
is
more
than
most
have.

VIII. Immolate
your
heart.

ON SOME STREETS

The children don't wave
to cops. Instead, they stare,
eyes glinting—an array
of hard, black diamonds.
Sallow skin. Sparse freckles.

Front-yard autos
hiked up on make-shift
stilts. A chow dog
wandering loose, patches
of fur hanging off his belly.

Each young face turning
to watch the patrol
car's path on the block.
Each face hardened
into a cold, white cipher.

BUCKET-HEAD

In an ideal world,
we all would've felt
sorry for him—a
tall white-boy LT
assigned to Investigations
since he was too
incompetent
for Patrol. He

got to wear a suit
and tie, though,
and meet behind
closed doors on the
carpeted second floor
with the Chief. We

all knew he'd burn us
in a heartbeat
to make himself
look good. You could
tell by the way
he galloped
down the hall,
staring off
in the distance,
frowning. Always too
busy for a hi or a bye.

One tight breath
curtailed inside his
chest—a permanent inflation—
as he strode hallways
and stairs. His

thinning hair ruffled
into a cocked curl
between premature
bald spots. When

I shot Expert
the second time
he was always
too busy
every day each day
for six months
in a row
to issue my Expert
pin. That's the
kind of guy
he was. Busy.
Real busy.

LEGS

I.   Navy cloth-coated
and muscular. Trousers
sharply creased, boots
at a high gleam.

II.   Chasing a car burglar
through a field of tall
crab grass. Tripping,
falling into weeds' pinions.

III.   Pumping. Nightly, mandatory
three-mile run. Our one
fat guy falling behind.
Walrus moustache.

IV.   Ragged jeans. Badge and police ID
concealed. Working undercover,
unshaven, slouching like a turd,
walking sloppy in torn sneaks.

V.   Up the Academy's metal stairs, chased
by DI yelling, "Faster. Move it.
Faster. If I catch you, it's down
for thirty." Handrails untouched.

VI.   Four sets of trousers up a winding
staircase. Guns drawn. Possible
suicide phoned in by IRS. Unopened
stacks of mail. Casino letterheads.

VII. The legs I'll never see. Yours,
beneath sharply creased,
navy trousers. Yours, exquisitely
muscled. Yours, at work.

CREWCUT

One man's neck
rising from creased

uniform shirt. Each
stiff hair on his head

defined by clippers
in some barber's steady hand.

Barely measurable growth
shorn into abrupt precision.

Ears covered by soft, rosy skin.
Only vulnerable, only visible

from the rear. Each edge
of hair, a sharp blade;

each curve of skin
adjoining, an invitation

to melt.

PHIL SAYS

*For Phil Bulone, Vietnam, January
1967-June 1968*

"Hundred and First
Airborne. Screaming
Eagles, Army." Vietnam
veteran tells me
this when I
urge him
to write about it:

"Some things I don't
want to remember."

* * *

I'll never forget
the nun. You see,
I was assigned for awhile
to a chaplain—Catholic
like me.

We helped him
distribute food,
clothes—that people
from the States mailed.

There was a sister.
A nun who helped
him. Taught the orphans,
was always smiling, always nice
to us.

One morning we went,

the priest was crying, tears
down his face. The translator
finally told us why.

The night before
the Vietcong cut
off the tongue
of the nun and left her
alive.

She'd said too many things
pro-American. Yeah,
I still got her picture.
Small. Black and white.

Her smiling. Before.

ONCE AGAIN

Deputy Darrell E. Lunsford, Sr.

How many times can I watch
the film of my cousin
getting killed by
three Mexicans running drugs?

The film of my cousin—
the family allows it to be used.
Three Mexicans running drugs
on I-10 East.

The family allows it to be used
for training purposes, showing
on I-10 East
yet another lawman killed.

For training purposes, showing
rookies how it happens quickly,
yet another lawman killed,
caught on grainy film from his cruiser's camera.

Rookies, how it happens quickly—
watch. Learn. So you won't be
caught on grainy film from your cruiser's camera,
and your family has to watch over and over.

Watch, learn, so you won't be
overwhelmed on the roadside and stabbed—
and your family has to watch over and over—
against the piney woods where we all grew up.

Overwhelmed on the roadside and stabbed,
you died, cousin,

against the piney woods where we all grew up.
How many times can I watch?

MIRACLE

Son, every time you show
up for court in your best
pressed uniform, saying, "Yes sir"
and "No sir" to the judge,
the prosecutor, and the slick-haired,
bargain-basement-suited defense
attorney who's already sold
his soul to the Devil—each
time, you're going to witness
an amazing transformation. The
low-life scrot who tried
to knife you, who fought
four officers, and had
ten pounds marijuana in his trunk—
that very self-same suspect has been transformed.
He has a good haircut and a shave.
Even his pimples now look innocent.
He's wearing an expensive suit and
a gold ring with a crest. Even he says,
"Yes sir" and "No sir," and every damn
friend, relative, teacher that he has
will go up on the stand and testify
that he's a "good boy," maybe
even on student council and the
honor roll, who absolutely couldn't
be a druggie or the violent no-count
who tried to kill you, do
you understand that, Officer?

RIDE-ALONG

Sgt. B.D. Soboleski

Another cop tells me
about the female
doing the Ride-along
when Sobo got killed.

Him lying there bleeding
bad; her, not knowing
to push the radio button
down when you talk.

That kid didn't shoot
her, even though he
knew she saw
the whole thing.

He stared at her
hard through the
windshield, holding
his gun, deciding.

She didn't even know
the name of the street
or the hundred block
to tell Dispatch.

So, once the kid ran
she crawled out
the shop to Sobo, turned
him over, held his hand, recited

the Our Father with him
while he died. This

other cops says
he heard she moved

out of Houston. Went
up East. Came back
to testify against the kid.
Had a nervous breakdown.

My Ride-alongs—I
show them the radio
button. Me—I
want an ambulance.

TWO CASES CHILD ABUSE,
SAME WORK WEEK

Each time I make a good
case. Document all wounds,
each scar. Bruises, bites or
burns. Get a crime scene
photographer. Sit on the floor
while interviewing the child,
like in the training videos. Make
proper notifications. Type
the report before going O.D. File
charges, knowing that
getting arrested
doesn't change
anyone's rot
or fondness for torture.

* * *

Soft pink to black.
Pale rose to livid purple.
Flesh to flesh, ruptured
families, dismembered hopes.

Torn fabric.

PENAL CODE UPDATES

Mister-Long-Legs-Encased-
in-Black-Starched-Wranglers.
Mister-Belt-Buckle, whose two-toned
ornate silver rectangle with swirled brass
inlays proclaims "Champion"—
a boxed advertisement riding
a flat stomach inches above your dick.

Since you barely speak at lunch
break, when the topic turns
to couch dancing, I take
the initiative, winking,
sliding eyes up muscled, tanned arms
before I speak, "With those
britches as tight as you're wearing,

I thought you'd be doing all
the dancing." I haven't spoken
to any other officer yet; the table stops
chewing. A cop to my left says, "He
don't know how to dance." You respond,
"I'm too shy," with a tinge of blush
but a steady appraising gaze.

Later during the afternoon training
session you extend those legs
across the chair between us. Shined
cowboy boots up to the ceiling.
Hand-stitched leather, rigid encasement
of toes, arch, heel. The taut stretched
skin at the top far too fragile for any touch.

BEFORE SHIFT

This surgeon training us says,
"Stomach wound. The best thing
you can do for a stomach
wound is not have eaten. It's

a hell of a lot easier
for me to fix you up
on an operating table
if your stomach is

empty when you get
shot." He laughs;
we laugh. What about
pumping chest wounds?

"Hey, you got a few
seconds on those. Pull
out your wallet. Find
something plastic and put

it over the bullet hole.
You got to stop that blood
spurting or you're dead
real fast. Maybe you got five seconds."

* * *

Before shift sometimes
we practice. Don't use
your regular hand. Un-holster
your weapon with the other

hand. Pretend your strong hand
has been shot away. Try
it. Stretch. See if you can
do it. Try. Reach. Reach.

HE'S THE ONE

you got assigned to
for deep nights
in FTO phases.
A short, fat

guy who routinely broke
department-issued holsters
by inserting a huge hand
against patent leather

at an angle unheard of
by the equipment manufacturer.
He boasted that he ate just once
a day, only one great big

meal each twenty-four
hour period. When
his nightly belching
rumbled warm from front seat

passenger side to front
seat driver's side, it
was so rich I swear
I tasted his meal.

One of the male trainees
in our group figured out
why he did pushups
every five A.M. against

the side of the vehicle.
He had a hard-on. All
I remember is his vast

weight rocking the patrol

car ever so slightly
and the considerable grunting.
Me at the steering wheel
slapping my face

to stay awake
the last hour
of the shift, while
day broke beautiful

across the empty cement
lot.

TIRED, HUNGRY, STANDING

in the same assigned spot
for ten hours. Standard
summer O.T. Sweat a steady
trickle off my tailbone,
feet pinned to greasy asphalt.

Another officer strolls by,
squat and muscled below
three gold chains and stiff
black crew cut. Eyeing the crowd,
we discuss weight lifting. How

it changes a man's body. He
first tells me to look for the wings
at the back of a guy's armpits. Then,
"Look at the titties," he instructs.
"They're big, real big, if a guy's serious."

Then he remembers I'm a girl
under my blue uniform shirt and silver
badge. Blushing, he turns away mumbling,
"Sorry." But I'm dissecting another
guy's bulges, pecs, delts, wings, jeans—
still zippered.

INVESTIGATOR'S PRAYER

Lord, take from me
her dark blue eyes
cloudy with fear
staring in a hospital
room beyond me, beyond
my uniform, nameplate, clipboard.

Make me forget
how I couldn't reach
her in whatever place
she'd found inside,
refusing to tell me
the name of her rapist.

Erase the smooth
helpfulness of the prime suspect,
her husband, as he bends over
her bed whispering, "Honey." Take
from me her mother's weeping stories
of childhood rapes and no one to help her.

God, lift from me the knowledge
given by all my training and guts
of who did it, of how
closely he lives with her,
how skillfully he manipulates
her, and how much she hides.

Silence the bell
inside me always
sounding, "I know he
did it." Lord, I don't have
proof, can't arrest him,

if she won't talk to me.

And every time on patrol
I drive by their house,
let her come out
if she needs me. Let
her believe I can help.

Make her trust.

FIELD TRAINING OFFICER

The skinny guy I'm training
this week talks
to his limp sandwich
before he eats it

each shift. I figure that
stint in the Army
on the tundra with no sleep
made him unusually social.

The last rookie loved
his Bible. Only
problem was it told
him women were pariahs.

He refused to follow
my orders. The lieutenant
set him straight, "In two weeks
she'll have a job; you won't."

The next batch has one
guy with a metal plate
riveted into his skull
after an auto accident.

His only dream
his whole life
has been to be
a cop. He drives

an unmuffled car
whose white sweeps
of busted quarter panels

vibrate from engine roar.

When he gets fired
all us FTOs wonder
if he'll break further
into crazy and try to kill us.

DILEMMA

We didn't talk
about the LT's face
not even out of the station,
or at the fuel pumps
at the end of shift. The other
supervisors refused to gossip

about it. We wondered plenty
though, passing him
in the carpeted hallway
under mean white neon,
eyeing the gouges haphazard
above impeccable uniform shirt.

It scared everyone
not knowing,
so we pretended
the deep, glistening red
that never healed
wasn't there. The

gashes wide open,
the blood suspended
between our air and his
disease. We couldn't
figure out how he
shaved or had sex.

No one really cared
if he might be dying.
We just wondered about
breathing the same
stale air that caressed
the fresh red jelly

on his face. We
hoped he wasn't
contagious
because he handled
our end-of-shift paperwork
and all our vehicle keys.

REPORTED DOG PACK

Following four summer-evening dogs,
telling Dispatch, "They're heading

north. Now west across
warehouse parking lot.

Going under perimeter fence."
One tawny female, her haunches

trailing sheets of wet ready.
Three males, happy and urgent.

Me, following orders,
in summer-slanted light.

AT THE READY

Our long trail of patrol car
overheads sped to a fight
in progress; over black
county roads the car
lights spewed a meteor's trail
of careening beauty. In the
trail of tail lights, no red
blaze of brakes, no silliness
of slowdown. Zero distractions.

Anticipation opened its fist
inside my chest.   Yes,

I've been trained.   Yes,
I prayed.   Yes, I squeezed
the twenty-six inch solid
hickory even as the Dispatcher
canceled the call
prior to arrival, and the solid
hickory slid back
into its holder.

Rotators off.
Wig-wag off.
Siren stilled
until the next fight
at the dance hall.

Until the next fight.

M.E.'S OFFICE

Everyone always hoped
there wouldn't be
an autopsy in progress
during tours for the rookies,

but that day, there was.
Me, the FTO. Three
rookies in tow. The cadaver
a black female adolescent.

Chest cavity sliced wide
open. White-coated attendant
suctioning the remaining blood
under layered fatty tissue

once called breasts. The
blond rookie from Canada
needing to excuse himself
from the everywhereness

of red meat, sawed-off
white bone of what was
once human and what
once was alive.

In the cold room
of unclaimed bodies, the
red-headed rookie asked
to look closer, was eager

to lift black plastic sheets,
stay longer, peer at minute
details. His rapt interest
pilfering human remains

on numbered trays. Wizened
agonies etched on charred
bones and skin. After this,
I knew which one I

trusted, which one was
decent, and who had a heart
inside the creased uniform
shirt, our common paradigm

of starched, thankless duty.

THE INCHES THAT MATTER TO ME

HEADQUARTERS

Remember that bowlegged guy
used to work on the third
floor? Had poofy blond
hair. Lived out in Spring.
Anyways, he started
screwing around on his wife.
Went on for months. She
finds out but he don't
know it. One day, she—
the wife—shows up
at Station One. Calls him
on the cell phone to
come down to the first
floor for lunch. Elevator
doors open and she
starts popping caps at him
with this little 'ole bitty .38
he'd bought her for
protection nights he wasn't
home. Boom boom boom
boom. Four or five times
and misses him each time
even though he's still
in that elevator and she's
standing less than three feet
back cussing him
out for cheating on her,
chewing gum the whole
time. Funniest thing
you ever saw. People
scattering every which
way not knowing if
she'd go after them

too. I bet all
firemen look the same
to a crazy female.
Thing is
she must've wanted
to miss. Ain't that
damn hard
to kill someone.

After lunch
we started
a jar to collect
money for shooting
lessons for the wife.

THE SECRET

Love whatever can save
your life. Your ballistic vest,
your razored reflexes. The
keys you rubber-banded
to keep from jingling. The
double-tied shoelaces that
won't come loose in a foot chase.
The short haircut a turd
can't grab in a scuffle
to ream your face into concrete.

                Love
that your nerves are a taut
high wire balancing a lovely,
sequined lady. Live on her
narrow steel day and night, on
and off-duty. Remember that
loser you arrested years ago
may be ready to collect your life,
as he vowed he would
some day. But, mostly,

                love
your gun. Practice drawing until
your arm is extruded machinery.
The big grip in your big hand
will cleave to palm, replacing all
other knowledge. Clean its high
performance parts as if you were
swabbing the chambered mysteries
of your own auricles and ventricles.

And

when you walk
the lawman's walk
into dirty danger, love
nothing, except
what will save your life.

TUESDAY A.M.

We almost took that call
but before we keyed up,
Jerry jumped on it—911
Hang-up. "No big deal"
everyone—including him—
is thinking. But when

he arrives, hysterical
W/F screams something
about husband shot
hisself, husband shot
hisself, and sure 'nuff
in back bedroom the son

'a bitch is dead from
bullet to head. Jerry
peels female off carpet,
calls for EMS, the ME,
and the Sarge. Female
is dead guy's wife.

Says husband was depressed
over losing job and didn't
go to job interview just
yesterday, so she got
pissed and exited house
articulating that she'd

spend night with B/M
friend. When she returns
around 0920 hours, hubby
has dispatched himself
outta his misery, one piece
of brain hanging from his

nose, like a shrimp.
Gun still in hand.
A little excitement
for all of us working
what's generally
a dead shift.

AWARDS BANQUET

for Deputy Craig Hughes

I don't wonder
about the wife, face down,
straddled by the husband
in a closet.

I don't even wonder
about the husband
angry or crazy enough
to want to kill.

I have questions
about the gun—its
silhouette against a dim
interior of hanging shirts,

a splatter of shoes.
Loaded or not, one of those
plastic fakes or real.
Maneuverability in a tight

space. And that one officer
yelling at him to drop it. The
husband complying, then
picking it up. The second

yell. Did the officer
remember his new baby
at home, the son
in first grade? Of

course not. He shot
and killed the right

person. Saved a life;
took one. Tonight

in a crowd of fellow
cops and spouses, he
gets a plaque, greying
crew cut shining in stage
lights. He stands
removed. Honored.
Alive.

ALCOHOL STING

One man's feet
in thin black flip-flops
behind the counter
in a small convenience store.

In thin black flip-flops
he stands, while I frisk him
in a small convenience store,
smelling of sweat, Pine-Sol, and wieners.

He stands while I frisk him,
a skinny Pakistani,
smelling of sweat, Pine-Sol, and wieners
saying, "Yes, Boss. Yes, Boss. Yes, Boss."

A skinny Pakistani,
watching me find the gun,
saying, "Yes, Boss. Yes, Boss. Yes, Boss,"
asking me to put on his other shoes.

Watching me find the gun,
he proclaims his innocence, still
asking me to put on his other shoes,
while I count the bullets.

He proclaims his innocence, still
standing and blinking behind ill-fitting glasses,
while I count the bullets
and he twitches his toes.

Standing and blinking behind ill-fitting glasses,
he asks permission to put on his shoes
and twitches his toes,

the crushed toenails like grey slate.

He asks permission to put on his shoes
as if he wouldn't have shot us.
His crushed toenails like grey slate—
one man's feet.

YARDSTICK

*It's all measured
in inches,* he says,
comparing the fire
service to street

policing. *When I got
certified to drive
the apparatus. I had
to park each*

*back bumper two inches
from a cement dock.
Had to back up all
forty-five feet to eighteen inches*

*from a pole I couldn't
barely see, using side mirrors.
Had to stop on wet and on
dry. Two licenses it took—*

DPS and departmental. He
smiles and drifts into years
of nights on a ladder truck. And
I reach for the inches

that matter to me.

SIX TIMES SHOT ON-DUTY

for Kenny

When this wife
makes love to you,
the scars don't matter.

You've even
begun to joke
about the scrot
who fired out
his driver's side
window and hit
your left hand
on the steering wheel,
after the Academy
instructors had
said, "Hell, it's
an impossible angle
in a pursuit, so
don't worry." The

other times? They don't
even inhabit your dreams
anymore.   This wife
follows the road map
of squiggled flesh
and bumpy scar tissue.
She discerns the trail,
its buried pain, the
need for her searing
beauty, and, you hope,
the gratefulness
in your career-hardened heart.

DOG REMEMBERS NIGHT

We're crawling up
this hill and the guy
who just killed Ericsson
is holed up at the top, shooting.

Ahead to my left is a K-9
officer and his dog, both
belly-to-ground with us
after the cop-killer.

Then the handler stops
some rounds. I can see him
but can't get to him,
and he's not moving.

His dog sticks
his big muzzle
into the officer's bulk
and whines. I hear

the dog's breath
trapped in his strong throat
by the lump of love
or whatever it is bigger

that a dog feels for his man.
And the dog is whining,
whining a jagged blue line, his
breath more and more strained,

more and more squeezed
into a clean, high whimper,
the blood silvery
in the full moon's glare,

and then that poor dog stops
whining. He stops trying
to pull his handler back
into this world, and I know

that guy is dead and that
blood-stained summer concrete
is all that's left to that dog,
even as it chills and blackens.

TRUE LOVE

Your lover was separate
from the gun
he bought you,
or was he? Your first
cop boyfriend; your
first handgun.
                No one

else believed in your
calling to wear a badge
and police the streets,
and no one else would pay
for the six-shot revolver
required in the Academy.
                He said

he bought it off another
cop, from another cop
who had killed someone
with it, but a good kill--
justified, legal, no-billed.
                Your first

intro to heat-tempered steel,
a stiff cylinder release, the shiny
promise of undimpled primers, the
dire necessity of chambered
rounds, the scorching ejected brass.
                You still

own the L-frame 357 magnum.
Your first stainless tool for
survival, more cherished, more

solid than the freckled,
flat-topped cutie who gave it
                    to you.

FEELING TOO MUCH, AT TIMES

LIFELINE

Dispatch is your mother. The one
voice that replaces everything
in your existence. The one
whose impartial formulaic syllables
steer you
into vast unpredictable danger
and ferry you out again.

Even the voice of your Sarge
or your LT won't bend
for you.　　　　But
Dispatch cares; Dispatch alone
times your walk into houses
with unknown weapons
and intox, while the caller
screams into the promise
of a phone line manned
by a steady, dispassionate voice.
Your own cold swim
back to the safety
of your patrol car
braced by the Dispatcher's
tempered voice.

　　　　　　No
matter where you are,
or what is interrupted, when
you hear
the Dispatcher's voice,
you'll respond.

WORKING FUNERALS

you see how quickly
life becomes death,
surprising everyone. You
glance at the grieved,

her bereft heart beneath
the shapeless black rayon,
her heart huddled
against itself. Watching

cars turn in, you
see men's upright
suited discomfort. You
ask yourself if his widow

notices it's a cloudless
springtime day, and you
already know the answer
because you finally love

a good man too.

GAS STATION

You could lose
your life here
in the white
glare of mean
neon, before
the barred windows
and doors release
oily breath
over stained concrete
and gnawed chicken bones,
before a passing
driver sees
the slumped basket
of your loosened bones
and bleeding muscles.

You think this
every time
you drive
by this jeweled box,
gaudy with threat,
gilded in filth,
girded in posters
of block print
warning, Illegal
Arms, Illegal
Consumption, Illegal
Possession. You hope
someone else will
die here. Not
you. Not this
night.

WITNESS

All our desks sit
on grey industrial
carpet behind heavy
glass doors. At

the next desk
over he sits
talking. His voice
a honeyed, coaxing

rumble spreading all over
this new chip. Both
his big hands cradle
a tiny silver phone

enabling him oral
seduction at 0800 hours
sitting at a wooden desk
next to me. Does he

think we can't hear, don't
care, won't ask out loud
about the wife pictured
in a flowered pewter frame?

The wooden desk
the other side
of his has a book jacket
garish with an angry-looking,

fake aborted fetus. My
desk is stacked
with Crime Prevention

brochures. Glossy ads

for safety that can't
prevent a damn thing.
His desk is empty,
slick. Varnished

countless times. Hard
enough to ricochet
feelings. So, we have
none. Figure that

female he's sweet-talking
will find out soon
enough about the wife.
It'll turn out alright

if neither female carries
a gun.

WESTHEIMER AT COMMONWEALTH

Years ago some skinny guys
lived in that tiny, neon green shack
on Westheimer near the steady steam
of boy prostitutes, sultry teens
in fresh tattoos, and prancing transvestites
in study high heels. Those

guys stayed deathly
pale with oily, brown hair
tucked behind ears, and occasionally
one of them would mow
their miniscule patch of yard. Jerky
shoves behind a small push mower,

half-hearted and barely enough to irritate
crab glass claws in the dying
St. Augustine. I drove by one day
and saw a guy mowing. Tall
and lanky, greasy jeans hung
with thick chains and doo-dads,

shirt off. His thin frame
straining to push that small push
mower across the wide front porch,
where he was mowing the dark-green
Astroturf in short sweeps of sweaty effort,
ribs heaving and brow furrowed,

vacant eyes steady on the horizon.

SOLVENT

We caught a run
to a complainant-reported
chimney fire when I
was chauffeur on 51s
pumper. Crew of four.

Complainant dazed in his
sunken living room. Said
his chimney caught fire
when he was cleaning
the soot with gasoline

and a wire brush. Black
stuff came off real good
at first 'til wire bristles
sparked and complainant set
his face, his chimney, and

his big wire brush on fire.
The four of us busting
our guts trying not to laugh
at subject idiot who said
he was an engineer, who lived

in an expensive house, who
had singed off his eyebrows,
eyelashes, and most his beard. We
just kept saying, "Yep, could've
happened to me. Yep, hard

to remember these things. Why
don't you get some salve
on your face, and we'll call

an ambulance." First
and second degree burns.

Near-fatal case
of the stupids.

TRICKED-UP

First time we saw
that car in the lot
we thought it belonged
to the big dog himself.

Its shiny black wax job
reflected high-vapor sodiums
so bright you'd go
blind just walking up

to it. All the windows tinted
more than legal dark. Four
antennae radiating stiff lethal
from the trunk's metal midnight. A

back seat that could hold
plenty of secrets in its plush
folds. The custom steering wheel
a real man could use to subdue

asphalt, cement, or a good piece
of ass. Then, we found out
the car belonged to the new guy
whose policing career has already

spanned several sheriffs. The
guy with the fancy haircut
whose flat ass isn't yet
balanced by a beer gut. But

whose thin lips
would love to arrange themselves
into a deep, hard kiss

and whose swagger is a little

too pronounced to be caused
by his cowboy boots. Each grin
a calculation in cute, fervent
masculinity. Thank God,

his male radar
hasn't picked up
us females
he's working with

tonight.

JUVE COURT BAILIFF

Inside nicked white walls
and grey ceiling tiles
held up by my armed boredom,
a couple sits.

Her pouting, dark beauty
nestles inside
the tender crook
of his taller shoulder.

She dozes, full
red lips parted
until her name is called.

Walking up to the judge,
the pregnant mound
sways inside
her denim shift.

I hear she's sixteen. Minor
in possession of cigarettes.
I hear the man
is her father.

His bald, sunburnt head
and soft, large body
yearn towards her. An
intent, begging envelope

of a much older man. Sullen
and angry, she refuses,
flicks black hair away
from her face. Pouts

and turns away
from his pleading. Rubs
her protruding belly
as he smooths her hair.

After the Class C sentencing,
they sit. He keeps fingers
on the sheets
of her long hair.

She sleeps.

WOODHEAD AT PORTSMOUTH

That corner belonged
to them—large-jawed,
blonde women in flowing batik
tops and their men.
Parked motorcycles
in scattered shiny metal
across the front yard.

Every summer's night
the women sat on cement
front steps eyeing the passing
cars, big knuckles around one
more beer, gold hoop earrings
flashing territorial imperative
backed by flinty stares. Claiming

that corner by crushed
beer cans lobbed onto the lawn.
Claiming the burly, bearded men
belonging to the bikes. All of them
sitting next to
the tall palmetto's
dark-green stilettos

against warm sky's belly.

POEM FOR A DYING OFFICER

Watching him wrench unsteady
legs from a small maroon pickup
and crunch through the muddy ruts
of a shell parking lot we're paid
to protect, or watching him light up yet
another cigarette and exhale
smoke the dun color of his skin, I
think when was it we grew
acceptance of slow death?
                    Imagine him
a sturdy young man with sound lungs,
wide pink bladders cupping
his glad air.   Imagine him
in the Westside shootout, running,
scattering lead. Although, even I
know that what I think of him
and his dying doesn't matter—
when I can't change him or stay
his summoned guest. In the harsh
headlights, the shallow planes
of his cheeks and stained fingers
are already tinged blue.

            Friend,
how it is with your swathed heart
I don't know, but mine feels
too much, at times.

SHE DIED

in the middle
of a phone call
to her adult daughter
in some other state.

Elderly and upstairs
in a modest gray bedroom.
Fully clothed. The body
transport guys relieved the

stiffening left leg would still
straighten. One black-suited
guy pumping the polyester-knit
clad leg into an angle

parallel to the gurney
they almost dropped
at the sharp bend
in the carpeted stairway.

Her cat pacing through
rooms, pushing heavy doors
open. Mute. The scenes
I didn't see a week earlier

when my own mom died.
July's heat incising backs,
heads, hands, shoulders.
Asphalt oozing

black in every intersection,
ruining boots, staking this one
summer's territory
indelibly in heart.

PRAYER OF AN ARSON INVESTIGATOR

God, I want to understand many
things on this side
of Death's yawn. I want
to comprehend how a man
beats his wife.

Impacts of her body hurled
against an apartment's sheet rock
walls. The screams. His cursing.
I want to understand the silence later
suspended in night's dark stretch.

And when it starts again
inside him inside her
I want to understand her
body's heft into linoleum tiles
until she quits moving.

Lord, let me acquire something --
wisdom, grace, compassion --
when he place her unconscious
in the tub, pours
gasoline, and sets her on fire.

Most of all, Great God, let
me understand
neighbors who hear it
all and never call
the cops.

EXPLOSION

Texas City, 2006

This one guy (white male) was concocting
    a bomb in his narrow bedroom

in a carpeted, first-floor apartment,
all-beige. One roommate,

male, sitting next to him at a desk. Both
    dirtbags since knee-high. Blue plastic bowl

in his lap full of a white powder
    he doesn't know is highly unstable.

He's mixing it with both hands, fingers
    extended, after reading Internet recipes,

and—ka-boom—he gets thrown
    back on a twin bed, while all glass

in patio doors and plate windows
    blows. Skinny, white mini-blinds

land on a fake-rustic, grey fence in front,
    now broken and leaning. Hysterical, but intact,

roomie calls 911, altho' he's a bomb-maker
    too. Stupid is laid out, external

genitalia missing, both hands
    gone, skin so scorched

he could now quality for EEOC
    corner at the dinner table. Pounds

and pounds of white explosive
powders heaped in closets, the kitchen,

next to socks, briefs, and Pepsi cans.
The Feds had to evacuate and detonate

the entire apartment complex, 'cause
they couldn't ID all those unlabeled

powders which shone real pretty, come to think
of it,when I lit them up with my flashlight.

SERIAL KILLER

Sometimes I remember how
he carted the bodies frozen
across interstate cement
in his truck's refrigerated maw.

Other times I see girls
like the ones he selected—
runaways already married
to danger, a past that bore

no repeating. Slender girls
with large dark eyes,
winsome above a boyish
flatness barely hinting

at a womanhood still
distant. What I pray
is that the first blow
was an outright kill.

That he wasn't too excited
to aim well and execute
swiftly before laying
each one out

inside his stainless tundra.
Rock-hard flesh and
frozen hair later
jettisoned into scrub

besides stagnant ditches
next to a highway's
curling cement ribbon

leading to the next

tender girl.

AT MY COUSIN'S FUNERAL

Everyone caught
by surprise—someone else's
plane, broad daylight,
good weather. Everyone

uncomfortable on a dead man's
furniture, watching his T.V.,
eyeing fishing portraits
in the narrow hallway, his wife,

his dogs. A young bull rider
talks to me, "There's a place
on the bull where nothing
moves. Hard muscle. You've got

to find it. Sometimes you see
a bull rider go back
and forth 'til he finds it. The
only spot you can sit

on during a ride." I nod
to the telling—three broken collarbones,
a pelvis. His recent ex
circles nearer—huge, curled bangs

rising above urgent, pouting
mouth. "You've got to be
strong enough to stay upright
when the bull goes down. Think

about it—not only do you
got to stay on when he bucks,
you want your face off

both of them horns when he goes

down." I wonder about my cousin's
final ride. No amount of strength
or thrust or prayer able
to lift a single-engine plane

spiraling downward into dirt.

KNOWLEDGE

In childhood I dreamed
intense moments of combat
in World War II. Muddy
fatigues and boots, drawn face
above khakis and close-gripped gun. A
soldier's brief delight found lighting
a Camel, airmail sheets with thin ink.

Today I tell a new friend
how much I yearned
to learn killing, warfare.
To be only and evermore
a boy fighting
among boys. He listens
and tells me this about Vietnam.

*The rules changed randomly. All
the time without notice. That
was the hardest part—what
worked once might not
five minutes later. Another*

*guy and I are with a Sergeant
one night. We come on ARVN
soldiers asleep when they're
supposed to be guarding the perimeter.
Sarge tells the other guy
who had the machine gun, "Waste 'em."
The guy refuses. The Sarge pulls out*

*a .45 and holds it to the guy's head
and says, "Do it or I'll kill you."
Now that guy is living somewhere*

with that inside of him. Count
yourself lucky you never fought
in a war, especially Vietnam.

I nod my head up and down,
and don't tell him I could've done it.

INHERITANCE

I walk through
racks of uniforms,
in thin plastic bags,
returned by other officers.

Racks of uniforms
pressed into smart creases,
returned by other officers,
labeled with each officer's name.

Pressed into smart creases,
jammed in this long closet,
labeled with each officer's name,
they wait for the next assigned officer.

Jammed in this long closet,
some shirts missing buttons,
they wait for the next assigned officer.
I see names of people long gone.

Some shirts missing buttons,
a lot of zippers busted out,
I see names of people long gone—
fired, retired, or dead.

A lot of zippers busted out.
No order to the numbers—
fired, retired, or dead—
34 Regular next to 38 Long.

No order to the numbers
in tanned, disciplined rows,
34 Regular next to 38 Long.

Then, I see the uniform.

In tanned, disciplined rows
of thin fabric, false skin,
there I see the uniform
of one of us recently killed.

Thin fabric, false skin
labeled with the name
of one of us recently killed
in heavy block writing.

Labeled with his name
(I can't believe it's here.)
in heavy block writing.
I push it aside.

I can't believe it's here.
I won't look at the size.
I push it aside;
I walk through.

THE PRICE

What does she notice,
that slender beauty
with the high voltage
smile, dating a veteran
Homicide detective?

Does she wonder what
he did on-shift yesterday?
That he ate his tacos
off a flimsy paper plate
on another woman's
dead stomach? Can she
imagine he chewed slowly,
assessing blood spatter,
point of entry, angle
of attack? Every item
dusted, printed, diagrammed,
recorded. Evidence gathered.
Maggots ignored.

Can she fuck a man
whose smile will never
rise to his eyes? Is she
willing to marry a man
whose life holds
so much
intentional death?

TODAY

if someone has to
unravel the evidence
at my homicide, let him be
a relentless, thorough

detective with no emotions
left to skew judgment, no
history of nasty divorces
or issues with the opposite

sex. Let him find all
the clues. The scraped flesh
under my trimmed nails. The
new neighbors who glimpsed

my killer's car, headlights
off in the long circular drive.
Don't let the street cops—
for once—kick around the brass.

And please, dear God, don't let
the gun I am killed with
be my own. And when the banty-cock,
bouffant-haired, three-piece-suited defense

attorney dresses up the defendant
in his first new suit, a
professional haircut and pinkie
ring, don't let the jury

be fooled by the sullen dirge
of the SOB's cheerless childhood
and pitiful choices. Make

the jury sicken at the photographs

of my maimed and disgraced torso. Help
them understand how he enjoyed
the killing, how he relished his
own flush of sick cruelty. And

when the verdict resounds, let it be
an eye for an eye, because even if
I'm dead, I'm still on the side
of justice.